THE CURE FOR SMOKING

How the Universal Law of Attraction Made Quitting Cold Turkey Easy!

Michael Lally

Copyright © 2018, 2009 by Michael Lally.

All rights reserved. No part of this publication may be reproduced, distributed, or transmitted in any form or by any means, including photocopying, recording, or other electronic or mechanical methods, without the prior written permission of the author, except in the case of brief quotations embodied in critical reviews and certain other noncommercial uses permitted by copyright law.

Printed in the United States of America

ISBN: Paperback: 978-1-948172-61-5
        eBook: 978-1-948172-60-8

Library of Congress Control Number: 2018943069

Stonewall Press
363 Paladium Court
Owings Mills, MD 21117
www.stonewallpress.com
1-888-334-0980

To my mother,

who believed in me during the darkest times.

Thanks Mom.

I love you and I miss you.

Contents

ACKNOWLEDGMENTS 3

CHAPTER ONE: Introduction 5
CHAPTER TWO: The Universal Law of Attraction 9
CHAPTER THREE: Preparation 11
CHAPTER FOUR: Quit Talking 15
CHAPTER FIVE: Visualization 17
CHAPTER SIX: Write It Down 19
CHAPTER SEVEN: Stop Smoking Aids 23
CHAPTER EIGHT: Triggers 29
CHAPTER NINE: Stress 33
CHAPTER TEN: Today Is the Day 37
CHAPTER ELEVEN: Exercise 45
CHAPTER TWELVE: Summary 47

ACKNOWLEDGMENTS

I would like to thank my friends and colleagues, Mark Davis, Bob Keegan, and Jack Davis, for their constructive criticism. I would also like to thank my friend Larry Mulrine for his encouragement and considerable computer support. To Melissa Bevacqua, for her wonderful editing skills. To my good friend Lois Waelchli, for her moral support, direction, and guidance.

To Mary Pat Lally and Eleanor Sorick, for their encouragement and support, without which this book would never be. Finally, I'm grateful for the *Law of Attraction*, through which everything is possible.

CHAPTER ONE

Introduction

I have in the last twenty years lost over ninety pounds in six months; I quit drinking almost ten years ago, and I quit smoking and drinking coffee on the same day. I started smoking, like many people, because of a little curiosity, some peer pressure, and the arrogant thought that I would not become addicted. Eventually, I ended up smoking two packs of cigarettes a day for over thirty years. I tried to quit half-heartedly a few times and even tried the nicotine patch and gum. These methods worked for some people, but for many others, including me, they did not. I finally had success when I quit "cold turkey" and it was the easiest and fastest way to do it. "Cold turkey" is the process of quitting smoking without the help of smoking cessation aids of any type.

People have tried many different methods to quit smoking, from the patch, to different types of medications that make you sick if you smoke, hypnosis, and finally just plain old cold turkey. For me cold turkey was the fastest and the easiest!

There is no real *cure* for smoking. Smoking in itself is not a disease; it is a habit. A habit as defined by Webster's is an automatic pattern of behavior in reaction to a specific situation; it may be inherited or acquired through frequent repetition. As a smoker, you most likely have an addictive personality. Smoking is a symptom of that disorder, a disorder that is telling you that you need to smoke to feel better, to relax, or to concentrate. When we show you that you can do these things without smoking, then we have "cured" you of the smoking habit.

The Cure for Smoking

The method I call the "cure" I believe will work for anyone who truly wants to quit smoking. It is simple and easy to do. It doesn't involve medications or patches. People can be taught how to quit smoking. The *cure* does involve some strategy. I quit cold turkey by applying knowledge of the *Law of Attraction* I gained from the popular movie *The Secret* by Rhonda Byrnes, the book by Jerry and Esther Hicks titled *Ask and It Is Given*, as well as my own experience and observations of myself and others.

Using the patches and the medications are another way of saying, "I want to quit, but I don't want to have to do the work; I want the patch or the pill to do the work for me." I know people who had patches all over themselves; they looked like giant octopi were attacking them! They still had a cigarette in their mouth, not even caring about the risk of a heart attack. People seem to think the patch or the medications will take away the "memory" of smoking. They won't. Doing *anything* forty times a day for thirty years, whether it's smoking or eating ice cream, take it away, and a person is going to think about it. It's only natural. The patch or the pill will not create some sort of super willpower or amnesia to make quitting easy. *Quitting is easy*, if you know how.

CHAPTER TWO

The Universal Law of Attraction

This is the gift. This is the difference between the "cure for smoking" and the other methods used for quitting. The Law of Attraction is where the will power is. When used correctly, the Law of Attraction is the "cure" for smoking.

Since creation, universal laws have governed the universe and provide basic principles of life. They are laws of the Divine Universe. Universal laws apply to everyone, everywhere. They cannot be changed and they cannot be broken.

The Law of Attraction, of all the universal laws, is the most powerful. The simplest definition of the Law of Attraction is that like attracts like. Like energy attracts like energy. Desires are thoughts and feelings. Thoughts and feelings are energy, so what you think about, and how you feel about, those thoughts is what is attracted to you. In the physical world, opposites attract; however, in the metaphysical world, like attracts like. The Law of Attraction is always working. The Law of Attraction is neutral, meaning it does not distinguish between positive or negative thoughts. So it follows if you think quitting smoking will be hard, it will. Consequently, if you think quitting smoking will be easy, it will! The Law of Attraction is constant, and some of the ways I used it to help me quit were to change the way I *thought* about quitting, how I *talked* about quitting, *visualization*, the way I *felt* about quitting, and finally *writing* about quitting.

CHAPTER THREE

Preparation

Preparation is a very important part of the quitting process. This is the part of the process that will bring the Law of Attraction into play and make the rest of it easier. Just as with any project, laying a good foundation is very important to its success.

Do not set a date to quit. Setting a date will put undue pressure on you to quit at that time, even if you are not ready. It can lead to a failed attempt and unnecessary discouragement.

Many people have quit smoking cold turkey. One day they just decided they had enough and just quit. They claim they didn't prepare for that day, but I believe, if they were not preparing for that day on a conscious level, then they were preparing for that day on a subconscious level.

A person can prepare to quit smoking by changing the way they *think* about smoking. This is one of the key areas of preparation to make quitting easier. This area of preparation is done by reprogramming your subconscious mind. Many psychiatrists and scientists have said the subconscious mind is far more powerful than the conscious mind. It takes in far more information about the world around us. Fortunately, we can program the subconscious mind with the conscious mind, simply by the way we think, talk, look, and feel about things. The Law of Attraction works on vibrations. Everything in the universe is energy. Vibrations are energy. Feelings are vibrations. Therefore, feelings are vibrations, and like vibrations attract like vibrations. It is very important to *feel* the thoughts and the visualizations about quitting smoking. The thoughts alone may not be strong enough. A person can be thinking about quitting but still be giving off a *vibration* of not really wanting to quit. The type of *feeling* energy a person sends out to the universe is the type of energy to which it will be attracted. Like attracts like! In the case of smoking, if you feel you *can't*, then you can't. Consequently, if you feel you *can*, you will!

CHAPTER FOUR

Quit Talking

Another step in preparation is how a person *talks* about quitting. This is important because how you talk about quitting is a reflection of how you are thinking about quitting. Plus, it reinforces the thought process. You can't talk about it unless you're thinking about it.

I used to say things like *"I'm going to try to quit"* and *"I need to quit smoking."* This *talking* was a reflection of wrong *thinking*! By saying I was going to *try* to quit, I was leaving the door open to failure. It presented a kind of hohum type of attitude; if I quit, great; if not, oh well, I tried. On the other hand saying I *need* to quit puts too much pressure on myself and pressure is a trigger to have a cigarette. When I changed what I was saying about quitting to I *will* quit instead of *try*, and I *want* instead of I *need*, I began sending out a softer, more positive expression of my desire to quit smoking, to both my subconscious mind and the Universe. The more I used these words, the more I began to believe them; the more I believed, the more I began to *feel* I could quit. The more I began to *feel* I could quit, the more I sent out to my subconscious mind and the Universe my desire to quit. My subconscious mind and the Universe put me in position to get it.

CHAPTER FIVE

Visualization

Another very powerful way to prepare to quit smoking is *visualization*. For the longest time, I would talk about quitting smoking, but it didn't really begin to take hold until I started *seeing* myself smoke free. I would picture in my mind's eye how it *would* be to be smoke free. Even if I had to see all the way back to the time before I started smoking I would. I would envision myself doing all of the things I wanted to do without smoking. I would see myself not worrying if I had cigarettes. I would picture myself breathing better, jogging, running, or just walking up a flight of stairs without losing my breath. I would picture some of the benefits of being smoke-free coming true. I would see my teeth being whiter, my fingers no longer yellow, and my complexion getting a healthy glow. I would actually start to *feel* healthier, like one of those commercials for a soft drink, where everyone is happy and having the time of their lives because they have that particular soft drink in their hand. Visualization is a powerful way to program your subconscious mind and express to the Universe your desire.

CHAPTER SIX

• • • • • • • • • • • • • • • • • • •

Write It Down

The previous methods of talking and visualization are great ways to prepare to help change the way you think about smoking. An equally powerful—if not the most powerful—method of bringing the Law of Attraction to bear on your desires is *writing it down*. I use the following method, which I learned from the book *Ask and It Is Given* by Esther and Jerry Hicks. Writing it down is so powerful because it combines the other methods into one exercise. When you write your desires, you are bringing your concentration to a higher level. It helps you to relax and increase your focus. Writing also allows you to keep your focus *soft*, no pressure, so you can let it flow more easily and more freely out to the Universe. This allows the Universe to bring it to you more quickly. The more relaxed and focused a person is the higher the vibration. The higher the vibration, the faster the vibration will be received by the Universe. The sooner the vibration is received, the sooner the desire will be manifested. When I wrote down my desires, I would use *soft* phrases, because *soft* phrases offer less resistance to being received by the Universe. I would use phrases such as:

- Wouldn't it be nice if I quit smoking?
- Wouldn't it be nice if I quit smoking easily?
- Wouldn't it be nice if I quit smoking without the cravings?
- Wouldn't it be nice if I enjoyed quitting smoking?
- Wouldn't it be nice if I could enjoy all the money I would save by quitting smoking?

After a while the phrases changed to "*I*

know I can quit smoking easily," "I know I will quit smoking easily," and *"I know I can do it."* Let your thoughts go where they will while doing this exercise. These are some examples, but anything along these lines will express to the Universe your desire to quit without putting any undue stress or a timeframe on yourself.

I would write these types of phrases twice a day for about ten minutes at a time, once in the morning and once in the evening, if I remembered to do it! This process is so powerful, I used to have a cigarette before I wrote or sometimes after I wrote or maybe even *while* I was writing! It doesn't matter as long as the desire is being expressed properly. This isn't the end of the world, have fun with it. The time of day or how long you write is not carved in stone. Sometimes I would only remember to do it once a day, and some days I wouldn't remember to do it at all! That's the whole point. This is not something that is put on a timetable. There is no pressure to do it *right now.* These are suggestions that work, but they work in their own time! This is about preparing for when the time is *right.* There is no timeframe on this, no pressure for this to happen right now! For some it will be sooner than for others. What you send out to the Universe is what will come back to you. Send out positive vibrations about quitting, and you will get positive results. It will happen!

CHAPTER SEVEN

Stop Smoking Aids

Many people have fallen for the propaganda that quitting smoking was the hardest thing they ever did. Some people have smoked for so long they seem to be afraid to quit. They have forgotten how it was before they started smoking. They feel like they are alone or vulnerable, naked before the world, and will not succeed. Maybe they think they won't be able to think straight or some sort of uncontrollable rage will take over their minds, or who knows what else. Some people take the non-smoking aids because they feel they need a crutch to soften the cravings. They may have tried to quit before and didn't succeed; they lack confidence in themselves and do not feel they are strong enough to quit on their own. They turn to a patch, a pill, or a gum. They feel this will give them an edge. These things have worked for some people, but for many more they have not. Other people are lacking so much confidence they think the aids will give them some sort of super willpower. Others are just lazy; they expect the aids to quit for them. They think if they wear the patch, take the pill, or chew the gum, all the cravings will go away. Yet they are surprised when they get a craving.

Smoking is a habit. Habits are created by repetition. When you do anything forty times a day for thirty years, you *are* going to think about it from time to time! It's only natural. When someone gets a craving, whether they are using an aid or not, it is not something to get alarmed about. I even dreamed about smoking, but that's all it was, a dream! When people feel these urges or think about smoking while using these aids, they feel the aids are not working. And if they can't quit while using the aids, they don't believe they would ever be able to quit cold turkey.

What are the philosophies behind these non-smoking aids? There is a pill that is supposed to make a person sick when they smoke after taking this pill. We are already making ourselves sick because of the smoking habit. Do we really want to make ourselves sick because we gave into a habit? What are we saying to our bodies? That we care so little about it that we are willing to chance making it sick on a daily basis? When we get sick enough times, then we will quit! What is that all about? You are punishing yourself because you may give into a craving and have a cigarette. Talk about pressure!

The patch has a different approach to the problem. The patch works by administering a small dose of nicotine into a person's system through the skin. A person will still be getting a dose of nicotine without the need for a cigarette, thus feeding the addiction while eliminating the habit. Once the smoking stops, the person will be weaned off the patch gradually. Smoking is the habit. Nicotine is the addiction. The habit and the addiction have formed a bond. The addiction makes the habit seem pleasurable so the habit can feed the addiction. I have not heard of anyone developing a habit of wearing the patch or becoming addicted to it. I have heard of people wearing more than one patch at a time and still smoking. They are trying to overwhelm the addiction but are still giving into the habit. What they are doing while wearing the patch is like hooking an alcoholic up to an IV drip of alcohol, so they won't want to go drinking anymore. No matter how much alcohol they drip, the alcoholic will still want the sensation of "drinking." I haven't heard of anyone becoming addicted to an alcohol IV drip, although I've known a few people who wouldn't have minded being hooked up to the IV drip after they became alcoholic. The patch is still putting the drug into the system. The object should be to get the drug out of the system as quickly as possible. The faster the drug is out of the system, the sooner the cravings will stop.

The gum has a combination of solutions to the problem. Like the patch, the gum will provide a small dose of nicotine to help combat the habitual part of the smoking habit. It will also provide an oral stimulation. Some of the problems with this are the same as with the patch; another is the taste. It is a personnel choice, but I have found nicotine gum to have an unpleasant taste. For me chewing the gum would also stimulate one of my triggers to want a cigarette. When my mouth would start to water, I would want a cigarette. In the case of the nicotine gum, my mouth would water from the biological reflex of having something in my mouth, not the taste. The real objective should be to get the drug out of the system as quickly as possible, not to prolong the inevitable.

CHAPTER EIGHT

• • • • • • • • • • • • • • • • • • • •

Triggers

Simply put, triggers are a type of event or stimuli that initiate a certain type of response. A trigger can be anything from a time of day, a place, a food, a drink, or just plain old boredom. They cover a wide spectrum of things and are considered triggers as long as they cause a response. A good example of a trigger is the world famous experiment by Dr. Ivan Pavlov and his dogs. Every time Dr. Pavlov would ring a bell, he would feed his dogs. After a period of time, the dogs would associate the ringing of the bell with getting fed. When they heard the bell, they would begin to salivate, expecting to get fed. The trigger in this case is the bell. It can be the same with smoking. Some of the triggers I responded to were:

- coffee in the morning; two cups, at least four cigarettes
- driving in the car, depending on time and distance, every fifteen minutes, one cigarette, getting close to destination, another "quick" one
- after any meal, number of cigarettes varied
- work break, number of cigarettes varied
- a few drinks, number of cigarettes varied
- any type of perceived stress, number varied, depending on the amount of perceived stress

Triggers vary from person to person; what may be a trigger for one person will not necessarily be a trigger for someone else. One of the keys to quitting smoking easily is to know your triggers. Many of these triggers can't be avoided, for example, eating and drinking. When you are hit with these triggers, remember, The urge for a cigarette will go away whether you have a cigarette or not. This quotation is invaluable because of the truth in it. It was on a card my mother had from a Stop Smoking Seminar sponsored by either the American Heart Association or the American Cancer Society. Memorize this quotation, as it will be a great asset! Over time, the illusion that you need a cigarette will cease.

CHAPTER NINE

• • • • • • • • • • • • • • • • • •

Stress

One of the biggest triggers for almost everybody seems to be stress. Stress is the reason I tell people not to put a timetable on quitting. It will only put more stress on you. When a person sets a date to quit, they feel they have to quit on that date or feel as though they are a failure. This feeling of failure may set them back and give them the false idea that it may be too hard for them to quit. In reality, they just weren't ready to quit. Another reason not to set a date is because your timetable may not be the same as the Universe's. You can't tell the Universe when it's time. It will tell you. For some it will be sooner than for others; the key is to express your desire to quit and to let it happen. It will happen! When it does you will know it. You will change from wanting a cigarette to not wanting one just as much as you used to want one.

I used to try to time my quitting so I would smoke the last cigarette in my pack just before I went to bed. That way I wouldn't have any cigarettes around in the morning to tempt me and I would get off to a flying start. Good plan, I thought. Of course, it never turned out that way. I would always seem to have too many cigarettes in my pack to smoke them all before I went to bed. When I was close to having the right number of cigarettes to smoke, I would go and buy a pack. On those rare occasions when I finished my pack as planned, I wouldn't be able to sleep, worrying about waking up and not having any cigarettes. I put stress and pressure on myself to make it happen the next day, when I was not really ready. The amazing part of my quitting cold turkey is, on the day I quit,

I had three-quarters of a pack of cigarettes in my house and a full pack in my car! I just didn't want them. I think the fact that they were available actually helped me to quit.

There's a path next to where I live that winds through the woods for a couple of miles. Whenever I could, I would walk along this trail. It was during one of these walks that I made an interesting observation about myself. Usually when I took one of these walks, I would bring along a pack of cigarettes, in case I wanted to sit down and have a smoke while looking at the scenery (a trigger) or just have a smoke because it was "time" to have one (another trigger). I didn't think about it; it was a reflex. Most times I didn't smoke at all. When I started my walk and realized I had forgotten my cigarettes, all I could think about during the whole walk were the cigarettes! When I had cigarettes with me, I didn't notice them. When I didn't have access to them, they were all I could think about! In a way, when I did quit and the cigarettes were available it made it easier, because I felt I could have one if I wanted. I had a choice. I just didn't want one. In a way, I didn't feel alone. My companions for the last thirty years were there. I just wasn't going to smoke them.

CHAPTER TEN

• • • • • • • • • • • • • • • • • • • •

Today Is the Day

Congratulations! Today is the day you stop smoking. Be warned however that smoking will not go away without at least attempting to win you back. You *will* think about smoking. As I said before, do anything forty times a day for thirty years and you are going to think about it. It's only natural, so don't panic or read too much into it. If you drank five ice cream sodas a day for thirty years, you would think about that, too.

The next thing to remember is not to believe the lies that you are craving a cigarette; the drug generates these in your system. The more drug in your system, the bigger and louder the lies. That's part of the reason that people say the first three days of quitting are the hardest. The amounts of toxins in your system are usually at their highest when you first stop smoking. Your body; however, is constantly cleaning your system. After three days, your body is far cleaner than when you first started; therefore, quitting gets easier as time passes.

It's almost as if the addiction to nicotine is alive and needs a person to continue to smoke so it can exist. It needs nicotine to stay alive. It creates the illusion that smoking is desirable, even pleasurable, so it can get what it needs. It's smoke! How good can it taste? Its telling you that breathing in the burning residue of paper and tobacco is *pleasurable*. When a person continues to lie to you on such a continuing basis, you would no longer believe them, let alone associate with them. Why believe cigarettes? Remember the time you took your first inhale of a cigarette? For most people, coughing and lightheadedness followed it. The coughing and lightheadedness were your body telling you the *truth*. The more you ignored what your body was telling you, with each inhale the truth was being replaced with the illusion that smoking was pleasurable, until finally you forgot what it was like to be healthy! The little voice in your head telling you that you need a cigarette, that you can't relax or think straight or you could have just one, is telling you lies. Once you realize this and see smoking for what it really is—a dirty, smelly habit—you will take away some of its power. Remember, the urge for a cigarette will go away whether you have one or not.

I often hear people say smoking has a grip on them. This is another illusion. The person's thought processes have been reversed in a way, like seeing a reverse image in a mirror. In reality the person has the grip on smoking, not the other way around. The addiction has blurred their thinking in order to get what it needs. When you drop a pack of cigarettes, it doesn't jump up and sink its teeth or claws into your chest so you can't pry it off. When you drop a cigarette, it doesn't crawl up your arm, force your mouth open, and demand you light it. Nothing has power over you unless you give it power over you.

Your body wants to be healthy. How many viruses has it fought off? How many infections? How many wounds has it healed and broken bones has it repaired? Your body has rejected smoking from the beginning and is still rejecting it now. Why not give your body a little help? You and your body are a team. You're getting cravings because your body *thinks* this is what you want. It has been trained to respond to certain stimuli or triggers. Retrain it by doing something different when a trigger hits you.

For me, I quit drinking coffee, a major trigger for me, because I knew if I had a cup of coffee in the first few days when I quit smoking, I would have had a cigarette, which

I didn't want to do. Now I can have all the coffee I want and not smoke. I will *think* about smoking, but I will not *crave* a cigarette. There is a difference between craving a cigarette and thinking about smoking. The *thinking* about a cigarette is the habit and the *craving* is the addiction. The drug leaving your system causes cravings. Nicotine has told your body it wants nicotine. By smoking and reacting to the cravings in the past, you have reinforced this process. The cravings are the body's way of telling you the nicotine level is dropping, the same way it would tell you that you were hungry. Cravings only last a few minutes. The habit part of smoking is a memory, a reaction, or reflex to a trigger.

An effective method to counter the cravings is to tell yourself you will have a cigarette in an hour. At the end of the hour, if you still want a cigarette, tell yourself again that you'll have a cigarette in an hour. This relieves the pressure some people feel. A person feels relief is only an hour away and can usually handle an hour. Most people will be able to handle an hour without a cigarette; they do it all the time at work. Some people get caught up in the thought of never having a cigarette again, and this thought overwhelms them. When a person breaks quitting down into smaller more manageable periods of time, it becomes easier. They can break it down into even smaller time periods if necessary; if an hour seems too long, then put a couple of ten minute periods together. Build up to an hour, then a day. Create a system that is comfortable for you.

What if you have a cigarette? So what! That's the whole point: If you give into the cravings, so what! Don't beat yourself up over it. You just lost one battle. Many people have one cigarette and give up, saying, "I had a cigarette, I can't do it, I tried, and it's just too hard." A person having a cigarette hasn't broken some type of quitting "rule." Where does it say having a cigarette means you have to stop quitting? This is another lie by nicotine.

So you had a cigarette; don't be so hard on yourself! It was just a cigarette! Treat yourself with more kindness and compassion than that. If it were a friend who broke down and had a cigarette, most people would tell them it was okay, it was only a cigarette, and don't give up. Why don't people show the same compassion for themselves? Love yourself and give yourself credit for the progress you have already made. People say the United States lost the Vietnam War, but the North Vietnamese never won one major battle in that war. Just like smoking. One cigarette is only one battle. Quitting is the war! Keep going. Give yourself credit for the time you didn't have a cigarette. You *won* those battles!

People have been led to believe quitting smoking takes some sort of fantastic willpower. It doesn't. All it takes is some desire, preparation, and a belief in yourself and Universal Laws. It doesn't matter what the desire is. Universal Laws must be obeyed, and the Law of Attraction will put you into a position to have it come into your life. Once you realize this, the rest is easy!

CHAPTER ELEVEN

Exercise

Exercise is not necessary to quit smoking. Some people believe exercising helped them to quit. If so, great; whatever works for you. Exercise will provide you with an opportunity to see how much smoking has taken away from you in terms of level of endurance and exertion. Smoking takes away these things in such tiny increments they are not even noticeable. Over time, these things build up, like pennies turning into dollars and sand falling in an hourglass. That's one of the reasons you hear people, especially young people and people who have just started, claim smoking doesn't affect their level of fitness.

A benefit of exercise is it will provide you with endorphins, those feel- good chemicals the body emits after an exercise workout. In a way, a conflict will occur between the desire for nicotine and the desire for endorphins. Usually, when a person starts an exercise program they are starting to seriously think about quitting smoking. It is recommended that you do not start an exercise program without first consulting a physician.

CHAPTER TWELVE

Summary

Like many people, I thought quitting smoking was equivalent to scaling a mountain. I believed there was no way I could do it. As I look back, it was surprisingly *easy*! Quitting smoking doesn't take a great amount of willpower; what it does take is *effort*— the *effort* consists of doing the exercises suggested:

- *Change the way you *talk* to yourself and other people about quitting from "I *need* to quit" or "I *have* to quit" to "I *want* to quit" and "I *will* quit."
- *Change the way you *think* about quitting from "I *can't* quit" and "It's *too hard*" to "I *can* quit" and "It will be *easy* to quit."

- *Visualize* yourself being smoke free, doing it easily and confidently.
- *Write* down your desires about quitting smoking. *See* it, *feel* it, and *know* it can happen.

Remember to show some compassion for yourself. Be kind and gentle; your body is your friend and cravings are only a natural reaction to the drug leaving your system.

People will not quit smoking unless the desire is there to quit. They can take all the pills, wear all the patches, and chew all the gum in the world, but if the desire is not there, they will not quit. When a person really desires to quit, they will put in the effort. The desire summons the Law of Attraction. The Law of Attraction will create the effort. The effort will create the willpower. The rest is *easy*!

www.ingramcontent.com/pod-product-compliance
Lightning Source LLC
Chambersburg PA
CBHW021159080526
44588CB00008B/420